Follow-the-Directions Art
Nursery Rhymes

BY DEBORAH SCHECTER

New York • Toronto • London • Auckland • Sydney
Mexico City • New Delhi • Hong Kong • Buenos Aires

Teaching *Resources*

For Hillary-Dillary . . .

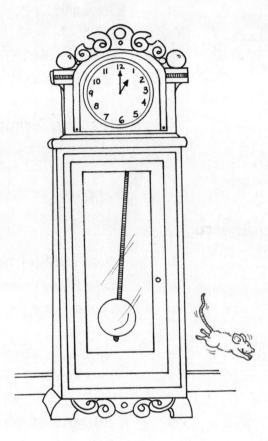

Selected teaching ideas in this book were adapted from
Follow-the-Directions Art Activities by Teresa Cornell and Amy Weaver (Scholastic, 2005) and
Teaching Reading & Writing With Nursery Rhymes by

Cover design by Jason R
Interior design by S
Interior illustrations by Maxie Chambliss, Kate Fla

ISBN-13: 978-0--545-1
ISBN-10: 0-545-102

Text © 2009 by Deborah
Illustrations ® 2009 by S
Published by Scholastic Inc. All rights rese

1 2 3 4 5 6 7 8 9 10   40   16 15 14 13 12 11 10 09

Contents

About This Book

Nursery rhymes—musical, rhythmic, and sometimes, silly—have charmed young children and captured their imaginations for generations. And educators know that the rhyme, repetition, and predictability of nursery rhymes make them natural motivators for helping young children build early reading skills. Unfortunately, many children entering school today are not familiar with these classic rhymes. Using the rhymes and accompanying craft projects in this book, you can help children revisit familiar favorites and introduce them to rhymes they may not know.

The simply worded directions for each craft project give children practice in reading and following directions, both essential skills in school and beyond. The activities also help children build math skills and concepts, including number sense, one-to-one correspondence, counting, directionality, geometry, simple fractions, making patterns, and more. Plus, children develop fine-motor skills and express their creativity as they cut, fold, glue, draw, and personalize their projects. (See Connections to the Standards, page 8, for more.)

After completing the crafts, children can use them as props when revisiting the rhymes. They'll enjoy helping the mouse in Hickory, Dickory, Dock scramble up and down the clock, counting the eggs in the Higglety Pigglety hen's nest, and making the cow in Hey, Diddle, Diddle jump over (or under, or next to!) the moon.

What's Inside

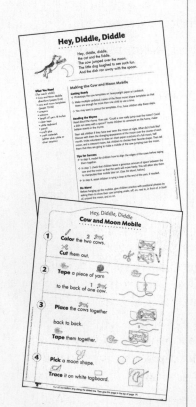

Each lesson includes the following features:

Nursery Rhyme The nursery rhyme sets the stage for the craft project.

What You Need This list details the materials, tools, and reproducible templates needed for each child to complete the craft.

Getting Ready Here you'll find setup instructions to do ahead of time, easy how-to's, and management tips.

Reading the Rhyme These ideas and discussion starters help you share the nursery rhyme with children before introducing the accompanying art project.

Tips for Success General tips and suggestions for leveling ensure that the activities go smoothly.

Do More These follow-up activities suggest ways to use the completed projects as props when revisiting the rhyme. Other ideas for extending concepts and skills are also included.

Student Directions Each reproducible mini-poster includes step-by-step instructions with large, easy-to-read print, simple text, key action words in boldface type, rebus-style pictures, and illustrations that show how the craft looks at each stage. Together, these features support children in following the directions and completing the projects independently.

Nursery Rhyme Tunes

Use the following resources to share with children the traditional melodies of different nursery rhymes (or make up your own). Singing the rhymes helps children build phonemic awareness, recognize rhyming patterns, and develop intonation and phrasing.

❁ Bus Songs
www.bussongs.com/songs/

❁ Just Playing: Nursery Rhymes and Other Silly Stuff
www.smart-central.com

❁ Nicky's Nursery Rhymes
www.nurseryrhymes4u.com

❁ *Teaching Tunes Audio CD and Mini-Book Set: Nursery Rhymes* (Scholastic, 2002)

❁ *Wee Sing Nursery Rhymes and Lullabies Gift Set*, Books and CDS (Price Stern, Sloan, 2007: reissue)

Reading the Rhymes

Begin by reading the nursery rhyme with children. For shared reading, write the rhymes on chart paper or write each line on separate sentence strips for use in a pocket chart. Laminate the rhymes so they can be written on and reused. Use wipe-off markers to highlight particular words or spelling patterns. Suggestions for using the rhymes to reinforce print concepts and build early reading skills follow.

❖ Provide background information for words or concepts that might be unfamiliar to children.

❖ Track the words with your finger or a pointer as you read each rhyme aloud.

❖ Model good reading techniques such as reading from left to right and crossing the text with a steady, sweeping eye movement.

❖ Point out punctuation, capital letters and other conventions of print.

❖ After reading aloud a rhyme a few times, ask children to join in for a shared reading. Invite them to tap the rhythmic beat by clapping their hands or drumming the floor.

❖ Encourage children to listen and look for words that begin with specific letters or sounds.

❖ Help children find rhyming words and guide them to notice that rhyming words can have similar and different spelling patterns.

❖ Ask children what they liked most and least about a particular rhyme.

❖ Since many nursery rhymes contain children's names, substitute children's names using self-sticking notes.

❖ If you write the rhymes on sentence strips, help children build sequencing skills by mixing up the strips for them to reorder.

SUPPORT FOR ENGLISH LANGUAGE LEARNERS

The characteristics of nursery rhymes that make them so useful in teaching young children to read also support children who are learning English as a second language. Authentic texts that follow certain patterns (repetitive, cumulative), and include devices such as rhyme, rhythm, and alliteration make text easier to predict and offer support for meaning construction. (Freeman and Freeman, 2007) The crafts made in this book also can be used as visuals and props to help make language and concepts more tangible for English language learners. Finally, the student directions for each craft offer extra support: they feature simple text, key action words in boldface type, rebus-style pictures, and detailed illustrations that show how the craft looks at each stage.

Source: Freeman, D., & Freeman, Y. (2007). *English Language Learners: The Essential Guide*. New York: Scholastic.

Preparing for the Activities

❖ To assemble the mini-posters that show the step-by-step directions for each craft project, simply photocopy the two pages of the poster. Cut off the bottom of the first page, then glue or tape it to the top of the second page, as indicated. Enlarge the pages, if desired.

❖ Highlight any color words in the directions in the corresponding color. You might also color some of the picture clues to match, for example, the color of construction paper children will be using.

❖ To make the reproducible templates sturdier, photocopy them onto heavyweight paper or cardstock.

❖ These activities work well at learning centers. Place the materials and tools needed for each project at a center. Display a copy of the directions so that one or two students at a time can easily read them. You might also post a list of materials needed for the activity so that children can check to see if they have what they need to begin.

Introducing the Activities

❖ Before children begin, discuss the importance of reading and following directions. Ask questions, such as "Why is it important to follow the steps in order?" Point out the numerals at the beginning of each step to reinforce the sequential order of the directions.

❖ Review with children the materials and tools needed for the activity (templates, precut pieces, paper, yarn, pipe cleaners, scissors, tape, glue sticks, and so on).

❖ Read each step and check that children understand what they are being asked to do. Review any text that may be unfamiliar. Help children focus on the key action words (in boldface type), such as *cut*, *fold*, *glue*, *tape*, and *draw*.

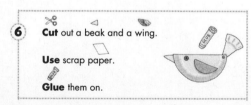

❖ Point out clues children can use to help them decode the text (rebus-style pictures above certain words, numerals, highlighted color words, and illustrations that show how the project looks at each stage). Children can use these elements as a guide to check that they are following the directions correctly.

❖ Model for children how to complete a project, showing them how it looks after each step.

Teaching Tip
To help children understand why the sequence of directions is important, try this: Cut the step-by-step directions for a project into strips, scramble them, and place in a pocket chart. Challenge children to put the steps in the correct order.

Tips for Success

❖ For very young children, you might precut templates and other materials or punch holes ahead of time. Specific leveling ideas for some of the projects appear on the accompanying lesson pages.

❖ If children are doing the activity with their own copy of the directions, you might suggest that they check off each step as they complete it.

❖ For projects that involve painting, cover the work surface in your paint station with newspaper or a plastic tablecloth.

❖ Some of the activities use paper plates and cups. Use the kind without waterproof coatings so that children can paint them.

❖ A few of the activities require the use of a sharpened pencil to poke holes. Supervise children when they are using the pencils or poke the holes for them.

❖ Encourage children to add personal touches to their projects! Have an assortment of craft materials on hand such as wiggle eyes, sequins, glitter glue, craft foam, pompoms, paper baking cups, craft feathers, and more.

Extending the Rhymes

Once children have completed their projects, they will enjoy using them as props when revisiting the rhymes. At a center, display a copy of the rhyme. Invite children to visit the center and use their craft to act out the events as they read the rhyme. Nursery rhyme projects that work well as props include:

• Lift-the-Lid Teapot (page 24)

• Peek-Inside Cupboard (page 27)

• Jack and Jill Puppet Slider (page 33)

• Hop-and-Stop Bird (page 36)

• Mouse Clock Climber (page 39)

• Royal Crown (page 42)

• Speaking Sheep Puppet (page 48)

Additional suggestions for extending the rhymes using the projects appear on the lesson pages.

Connections to the Standards

The rhymes, lessons, and activities in this book support the PreK–1 language arts, math, and art standards outlined by Mid-continent Research for Education and Learning (McREL), a nationally recognized, nonprofit organization that collects and synthesizes national and state K–12 curriculum standards.

Reading

- Understands how print is organized and read
- Uses mental images based on pictures and print to aid in comprehension of text
- Uses phonetic and structural analysis to decode unknown words
- Understands level-appropriate sight words and vocabulary
- Reads aloud familiar poems with fluency and expression
- Uses reading skills and strategies to understand and interpret informational texts such as written directions and procedures
- Uses reading skills and strategies to understand literary texts such as nursery rhymes

Math

- Understands that numerals are symbols used to represent quantities or attributes of real-world objects
- Counts by ones to ten or higher
- Counts objects
- Understands one-to-one correspondence
- Knows the written numerals 0–9
- Understands that a whole object can be separated into parts
- Knows basic geometric language for naming shapes (e.g., circle, triangle, square, rectangle)
- Understands the common language used to describe position and location (e.g., "up," "down," "below," "above," "beside")
- Sorts and groups objects by attributes (e.g., shape, size, color)
- Understands, repeats, and extends simple patterns

Visual Arts

- Experiments with a variety color, textures, and shapes
- Uses a variety of basic art materials to create works of art
- Knows the names of basic colors

Source: Kendall, J. S. & Marzano, R. J. (2004). *Content knowledge: A compendium of standards and benchmarks for K–12 education.* Aurora, CO: Mid-continent Research for Education and Learning. Online database: http://www.mcrel.org/standards-benchmarks/

Pat-a-Cake

• • • • • • • • • • • • •

Pat-a-cake, pat-a-cake,
baker's man,
bake me a cake
as fast as you can.

Pat it, and prick it,
and mark it with a *T*.
Put it in the oven
for Tommy and me.

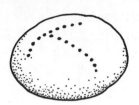

What You Need
(for each child)
- Initial Cake directions (pages 10–11)
- alphabet templates (pages 68–72)
- play clay, about 1/2 cup (see recipe below)
- 6-inch square of waxed paper
- sharpened pencil
- 3-inch square sponge
- tempera paint (various colors)

Play Clay Recipe
4 cups flour
2 cups salt
1 tablespoon vegetable oil
2 cups hot water

Combine the flour and salt. Add the oil and water. Mix well. Knead until the clay holds together. Add a little more flour if the clay is sticky, or a few drops of water if it is too dry. Store in a self-closing plastic bag. Makes enough for 10 children. (Make two batches for a class supply.)

Making the Initial Cake

Getting Ready
❖ Make the play clay ahead of time. (See recipe, below left.)

❖ Make enough copies of the alphabet letter templates so that each child has one for the initial letter of his or her name. Cut the letter sections apart along the outer dotted lines.

❖ On chart paper or a white board, list children's names in alphabetical order, underlining the first letter in each name.

Reading the Rhyme
Read aloud the rhyme, tracking the print as you read. Then reread it, inviting children to pantomime the action. Model how to trace the letter *T* on your hand when you read the phrase "and mark it with a *T*." Ask children to identify the name mentioned in the rhyme (*Tommy*) and the sound and letter it begins with /t/*t*. Reread the rhyme and use self-sticking notes to substitute the *T* and *Tommy* with children's first initials and names. As you read, invite children to trace the substitute letter on their hand when you say it. Then tell children that they are going to make pretend cakes and decorate them with the first letter of their names.

Tips for Success
❖ Have children make their cakes about 4 inches in diameter and 1/2-inch thick.

❖ Let the surface of the clay cakes dry slightly before children use their letter templates. This will make it easier to poke the holes.

❖ Make sure children understand that they should not taste or eat their cakes.

❖ Depending on room temperature and humidity, it may take a few days for the cakes to harden completely.

Do More!
Invite children to make additional cakes to label with letters they can use to spell three-letter words from the rhyme, such as *pat, put, man, for, can*, as well as other words.

Pat-a-Cake

Initial Cake

1

Roll a lump of clay into a ball.

Flatten it with your hand.

Place your cake

 on a waxed paper square.

2 What letter does

your name start with?

 Pick that letter.

 Press the letter

 on your cake.

Cut off this bottom strip along the dotted line. Then glue this page to the top of page 11.

(3) **Use** a pencil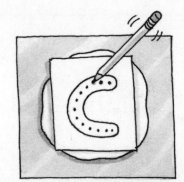

to **poke** through

 the dots in your letter.

(4) **Lift** off the letter.

Let your cake dry.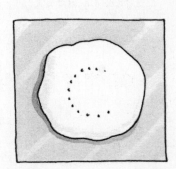

(5) **Use** a sponge square

to **dab** paint on your cake.

Pat-a-cake, Pat-a-cake

What did you make?

Your very own initial cake!

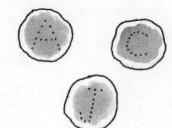

Follow-the-Directions Art: Nursery Rhymes © 2009 by Deborah Schecter, Scholastic Teaching Resources

Hey, Diddle, Diddle

Hey, diddle, diddle,
the cat and the fiddle.
The cow jumped over the moon.
The little dog laughed to see such fun.
And the dish ran away with the spoon.

What You Need
(for each child)
- Cow and Moon Mobile directions (pages 13–14)
- cow and moon templates (pages 72–74)
- crayons
- scissors
- length of yarn, 18 inches
- clear tape
- white tagboard
- pencil
- craft glue
- craft materials (glitter glue, white or silver sequins)

Making the Cow and Moon Mobile

Getting Ready
❖ Photocopy the cow templates on heavyweight paper or cardstock.

❖ Make multiple cardstock copies of the three moon shape templates so that there are enough for more than one child to use a time.

❖ You may want to precut the templates. If so, have children skip these steps.

Reading the Rhyme
Read aloud the rhyme. Then ask: "Could a cow really jump over the moon? Could a dish run away with a spoon?" Invite children to comment on the funny, make-believe events in the rhyme.

Then ask children if they have ever seen the moon at night. What did it look like? Discuss with them the changing appearance of the moon over the course of each month. Invite volunteers to draw on chart paper a picture of a full moon, half moon, and a crescent moon. Ask children to choose their favorite shape. Then tell them that they are going to make a mobile of the cow jumping over the moon.

Tips for Success
❖ In step 3, model for children how to align the edges of the cows before taping them together.

❖ In step 7, check that children leave a generous amount of space between the cow and the moon so that the parts will move freely. This will allow also them to manipulate their mobile later on. (See Do More!, below.)

❖ In step 8, assist children in tying a loop at the end of the yarn, if needed.

Do More!
Before hanging up the mobiles, give children practice with positional phrases by asking them to show their cow jumping *under, off, on, next to, in front of, in back of, around* the moon, and so on.

Follow-the-Directions Art: Nursery Rhymes

Hey, Diddle, Diddle
Cow and Moon Mobile

1 **Color** the two cows.

Cut them out.

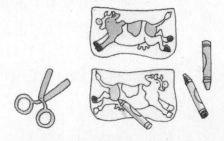

2 **Tape** a piece of yarn

to the back of one cow.

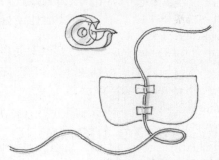

3 **Place** the cows together

back to back.

Tape them together.

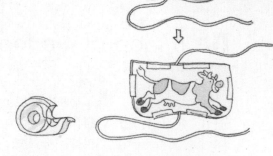

4 **Pick** a moon shape.

Trace it on white tagboard.

 Cut off this bottom strip along the dotted line. Then glue this page to the top of page 14.

13

Follow-the-Directions Art: Nursery Rhymes © 2009 by Deborah Schecter, Scholastic Teaching Resources

5  Cut out the moon.

6 Decorate both sides.

 Use crayons, glitter glue, and more.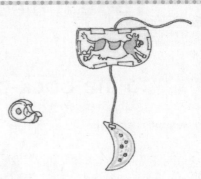

7 Tape the bottom end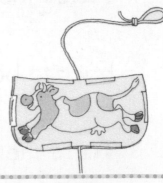

 of the yarn to the moon.

8 Tie a loop at the top

 end of the yarn.

Hang up your mobile.

Watch the cow

jump over the moon!

Follow-the-Directions Art: Nursery Rhymes © 2009 by Deborah Schecter, Scholastic Teaching Resources

14

Bedtime

· · · · · · · · · ·

The Man in the Moon looked out of the moon,
looked out of the moon and said,
"Tis time for all children on the earth
to think about getting to bed!"

What You Need
(for each child)
- Cozy Quilt directions (pages 16–17)
- bed template (page 75)
- assortment of one-inch paper squares in a variety of colors, designs, and patterns
- glue stick
- white paper rectangle, 3 by 4 inches
- clear tape
- half of a facial tissue
- photo of the child's face

Making the Cozy Quilt

Getting Ready
❖ Make copies of the bed template on heavyweight paper and cut them out.

❖ Gather a variety of papers for the quilt squares (construction paper, gift wrap, wallpaper samples, paper with different textures, and so on). Use a paper cutter to facilitate the preparation of the paper squares.

❖ Tear facial tissues in half lengthwise. Each child needs one half.

❖ Ahead of time, take headshots of the children in your class.

Reading the Rhyme
Read aloud the rhyme once and then reread it using a distinct voice and inflection to say the words spoken by the Man in the Moon. Invite children to join in on a rereading and echo your expression.

Then ask: "Have you ever seen the Man in the Moon? What did he look like?" Explain that the moon is far, far away in space and has mountains and craters on its surface. When viewed from Earth, some people imagine that these features resemble a man's face.

Invite children to share their bedtime routines and rituals. Do they take a bath? Read a story? Cuddle with a favorite stuffed toy? Then tell children that they are going to create a cozy quilt for a bed that they will personalize with photos of themselves.

Tips for Success
❖ In step 2, encourage children to arrange the paper squares in different ways before gluing them to the bed template.

❖ Assist children in writing their names on the blank line at the end of the directions.

Do More!
What time do children go to bed? On chart paper, create a simple graph to record children's responses. Ask questions, such as "What is the earliest time some children in our class go to bed? The latest? How many children in our class go to bed at [   ]? What time do most children go to bed? Extend the discussion by talking about the importance of getting a good night's sleep.

Cozy Quilt

1  **Count** 12 paper squares.

Choose different kinds and colors.

2 **Use** the squares

to **make** a quilt.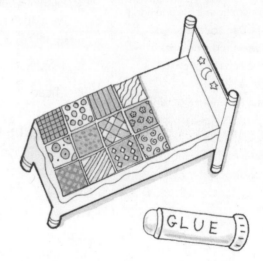

 Glue them to the bed.

3 **Make** a pillow.

Fold a paper rectangle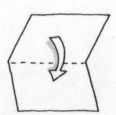

$\frac{1}{2}$

in half the short way.

 Cut off this bottom strip along the dotted line. Then glue this page to the top of page 17.

Follow-the-Directions Art: Nursery Rhymes © 2009 by Deborah Schecter, Scholastic Teaching Resources

(4) **Tape** the sides closed.

(5) **Stuff** a tissue inside.

 **Tape** the open end closed.

(6) **Glue** the pillow to the bed.

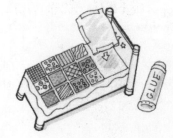

(7) **Glue** a photo of your face

to the pillow.

The Man in the Moon says,

"It's time for bed, _____."

Nighty-night!

Follow-the-Directions Art: Nursery Rhymes © 2009 by Deborah Schecter, Scholastic Teaching Resources

Twinkle, Twinkle, Little Star

Twinkle, twinkle, little star,
how I wonder what you are.
Up above the world so high,
like a diamond in the sky.
Twinkle, twinkle, little star,
how I wonder what you are.

What You Need
(for each child)

- Twinkle, Twinkle, Pasta Star directions (pages 19–20)
- dried pasta, assorted shapes and sizes
- 6-inch square of waxed paper
- craft glue
- glitter glue
- 8-inch length of yarn

Making the Twinkle, Twinkle, Pasta Star

Getting Ready

Cover work surfaces with newspaper or a plastic tablecloth, and provide moist paper towels for children to use for wiping glue off their hands.

Reading the Rhyme

Dim the lights and invite children to read or sing the rhyme with you as you illuminate each word with a flashlight. During rereadings, let children take turns shining the flashlight on the words and leading the rest of the class.

Before beginning the art activity, ask children to share experiences they have had viewing stars at night. Discuss how the rhyme compares a star in the sky to a diamond—a gem that sparkles and twinkles.

Tips for Success

❖ Pasta shapes that work well include long, spiral-shaped fusilli and rotini, and tubular penne and rigatoni. Rotelle (wagon wheels) are good for making star centers.

❖ In step 2, model for children how to squeeze a pool of glue about the size of a half dollar on the waxed paper. At least one end of each pasta piece should rest in the glue to ensure that the pieces are anchored when the glue dries.

❖ Assist children in labeling the waxed paper squares with their names.

❖ The glue should dry completely before children gently peel off the waxed paper.

❖ Children can paint their stars before applying glitter glue, if desired.

Do More!

Clip children's starry creations to a clothesline strung high across the classroom, or tack them to a bulletin board. Then invite the class to compare and contrast the different ways children formed their twinkly pasta stars. Encourage children to use descriptive words such as *shiny*, *sparkly*, *curly*, *spiral*, and *pointy*.

Follow-the-Directions Art: Nursery Rhymes

Twinkle, Twinkle, Pasta Star

1 **Practice** making a star using different shapes of pasta.

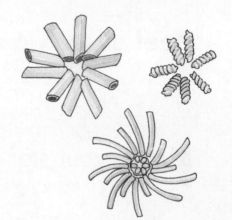

2 **Squeeze** a pool of glue  in the middle of the waxed paper.

3 **Make** your star.

Place each piece of pasta in the glue.

Follow-the-Directions Art: Nursery Rhymes © 2009 by Deborah Schecter, Scholastic Teaching Resources

 Cut off this bottom strip along the dotted line. Then glue this page to the top of page 20.

4 Let the glue dry.

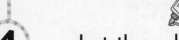

Peel off the waxed paper.

5 **Make** your star twinkle!

Dab on glitter glue.

6 **Turn** your star over.

Glue the ends

of a piece of yarn

to the star. Let dry.

Hang up your star.

Watch it twinkle

way up high!

20

Blow, Wind, Blow

Blow, wind, blow!
And go, mill, go!
So the miller may grind his corn.
So the baker may take it,
and into bread make it,
and bring us a loaf in the morn.

What You Need
(for each child)

- Whirling Windmill directions (pages 22–23)
- 8- or 9-ounce paper cup (uncoated)
- sharpened pencil
- two tagboard strips, 1 by 5 inches
- glue stick
- hole punch
- brad
- crayons

Making the Whirling Windmill

Getting Ready
Precut the tagboard strips that will be used for the windmill blades.

Reading the Rhyme
Before reading this rhyme, find out what children know about the wind and windmills. If possible, show them photographs of windmills. (To see a working windmill, go to www.goldenwindmill.org/videos/videos.htm.)

After reading the rhyme, explain that the wind makes the sail-like blades on a windmill turn. As the blades turn, they create energy that makes it easier for people to do hard work. Long ago, people used a windmill's energy to grind the hard dry grains used to make bread. Then tell children that they are going to make windmills with blades that really turn.

Tips for Success
❖ In step 2, check that children turn the cup upside down before attaching the windmill blades.

❖ Invite children to color the windmill blades before attaching them to the windmill, if desired.

❖ Assist children in punching the hole in the glued windmill blades and in attaching them to the cup.

Do More!
Once children have had a chance to see their windmills in action, help them learn how modern-day wind turbines are being used to harness the wind's power to produce energy in an environmentally friendly way.

Blow, Wind, Blow
Whirling Windmill

1 **Poke** a hole

near the bottom of the cup.

Use a pencil.

2 **Turn** the cup upside down.

This is the mill.

3 **Make** the windmill blades.

Glue two tagboard strips

together to make an X.

Cut off this bottom strip along the dotted line. Then glue this page to the top of page 23.

22

Follow-the-Directions Art: Nursery Rhymes © 2009 by Deborah Schecter, Scholastic Teaching Resources

4 **Punch** a hole

in the middle of the X.

5 **Use** a brad to put

the windmill blades

on the cup.

6 **Decorate** your windmill.

Draw a door and windows.

Blow, wind, blow—

Use your finger to make

the blades on your windmill go!

I'm a Little Teapot

I'm a little teapot,
short and stout.
Here is my handle,
and here is my spout.

When I give a whistle,
hear me shout:
"Please tip me over
and pour me out"

What You Need
(for each child)
- Lift-the-Lid Teapot directions (pages 25–26)
- three 8- or 9-inch paper plates (uncoated)
- scissors
- stapler
- brad
- paint, stickers, buttons
- craft glue
- tea bag

Making the Lift-the-Lid Teapot

Getting Ready
You may wish to precut the teapot front and lid in step 1 and the spout and handle in step 2. If so, have children skip these steps.

Reading the Rhyme
After reading the rhyme several times, encourage children to sing it with you and act it out. (To hear the tune, go to kids.niehs.nih.gov/lyrics/teapot.htm. This web page also includes additional lyrics and describes the accompanying motions.) Then tell children that they are going to make teapots to use for acting out the rhyme in another way.

Tips for Success
❖ For very young children, simplify this project by doing steps 1 and 2 ahead of time, or by eliminating the cutting in step 1 and having children simply draw a line across the plate to suggest the lid. Then have children skip steps 5 and 6.

❖ In step 1, model for students how to cut off about one third of the paper plate to make the lid.

❖ Instead of giving a third plate to each child, one plate can be used to make several spouts and handles.

❖ In step 3, check that children put the plates together face to face (convex sides facing out).

❖ In step 4, assist children in stapling the spout and handle between the two plates.

❖ Show children how to let the tea bag's string and tag hang outside of the closed lid.

Do More!
To turn their teapot into a handy holder, children can staple all the way around the teapot base to close it. Invite children to write notes to place in their classmates' teapots.

Follow-the-Directions Art: Nursery Rhymes

Old Mother Hubbard
Peek-Inside Cupboard

1 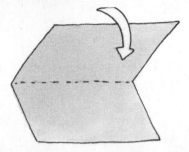 **Fold** the paper $\frac{1}{2}$ in half the short way.

2 **Make** two **2** cuts in the folded side.

3 **Unfold** the paper.

Cut along the fold.

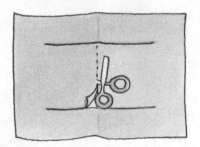

4 **Fold** the two doors back. **2**

Then **close** them.

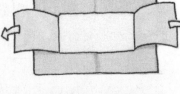

 Cut off this bottom strip along the dotted line. Then glue this page to the top of page 29.

28

Follow-the-Directions Art: Nursery Rhymes © 2009 by Deborah Schecter, Scholastic Teaching Resources

I'm a Little Teapot
Lift-the-Lid Teapot

1  **Make** the teapot front and lid.

 **Cut** a paper plate as shown.

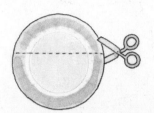

2 **Cut** a spout and a handle from another plate's rim.

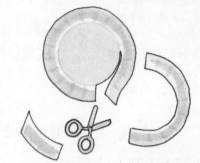

3 **Place** the teapot front

face to face

with another plate.

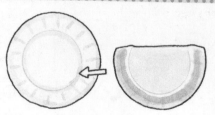
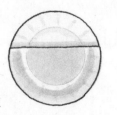

4 **Staple** the spout and the handle **2** between the two plates.

 Cut off this bottom strip along the dotted line. Then glue this page to the top of page 26.

25

Glue this page to the bottom of page 25.

5  **Punch** a hole through

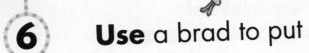 the lid and the plate.

6 **Use** a brad to put

the lid on the teapot.

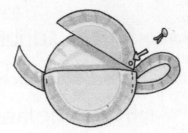

7 **Decorate** your teapot.

Use paint, stickers, a button, and more.

It's time for tea—

Put a tea bag

in your teapot!

Old Mother Hubbard

Old Mother Hubbard
went to the cupboard
to give her poor dog a bone.
But when she got there,
the cupboard was bare,
and so the poor dog had none.

What You Need
(for each child)
- Peek-Inside Cupboard directions (pages 28–29)
- 2 sheets of heavyweight construction paper, 9 by 12 inches (contrasting colors)
- scissors
- glue stick
- crayons, scrap paper, craft foam, plastic beads, and other craft materials
- grocery store food circulars

Making the Peek-Inside Cupboard

Getting Ready
You may wish to precut the doors in the construction paper (steps 2–3) ahead of time. If so, have children skip these steps.

Reading the Rhyme
Read aloud the rhyme and then during rereadings, invite children to take turns acting out the role of Old Mother Hubbard and her dog. Follow up by asking children to suggest what foods they would put in Old Mother Hubbard's cupboard. Then tell them that they are going to make a cupboard like Old Mother Hubbard's and fill it up.

Tips for Success
❖ To enhance their cupboard doors, children might glue on plastic bead "knobs," and raised designs cut from craft foam.

❖ Children might draw horizontal lines inside their cupboards to make shelves, if desired.

❖ After making their cupboards, give children grocery store food circulars to search for food items they would like to cut out and glue inside. Also invite children to fashion foods from scrap paper and other items. For example:
  - To make a wedge of Swiss cheese, they can punch holes in a triangle of yellow paper.
  - To make a dish of beans or pasta, they can glue dried split peas or broken spaghetti to a paper circle plate.

Do More!
Once children have filled up their cupboards, have them close the doors. Let pairs of children take turns asking each other questions to try to guess items that are inside. Or, have children take turns giving clues about one of the food items without naming it.

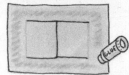

5

Turn the cupboard over.

Put glue around just the edges.

6

Place a sheet of paper

on top of the cupboard.

Line up the corners.

Press the pages together.

7

Turn the cupboard over.

Color and **decorate** it.

Fill up your cupboard!

Draw and cut out pictures

of foods to go inside!

Follow-the-Directions Art: Nursery Rhymes © 2009 by Deborah Schecter, Scholastic Teaching Resources

Rub-a-Dub-Dub

Rub-a-dub-dub,
three men in a tub.
And who do you think they be?

The butcher, the baker,
the candlestick maker.
And they all sailed out to sea.

What You Need
(for each child)
- Rocking Tub directions
  (pages 31-32)
- 9-inch paper plate
  (uncoated)
- 6-inch plate half
  (uncoated)
- tempera or watercolor
  paints (blue and a variety
  of other colors)
- paint brushes, one for
  each color
- 3 wooden craft spoons
- fine tip markers
- craft materials (yarn,
  paper baking cups,
  construction paper scraps)
- craft glue

Making the Rocking Tub

Getting Ready
❖ Prepare the plates. For step 1, fold each paper plate in half. Then cut scallops along the fold between the two rims. For step 2, cut small paper plates in half.

❖ Highlight the word *blue* in step 1 using a blue marker.

Reading the Rhyme
Read the rhyme several times and then invite children to chime in as you read it again. Point out the word *be* at the end of the third line. Explain that long ago, this word was another way to say *are*. Reread the rhyme substituting *are* for *be*. Ask children how this affects the rhyme scheme.

Next, discuss with children the three different careers described in the rhyme. Talk about what butchers and bakers do. Then explain that long ago, before electric lights were invented, people lit their homes using candles. Candlestick makers supplied the holders for candles that people used every day. When children do the art project, encourage them to use the information from this discussion as they decide how to decorate each of the three men.

Tips for Success
❖ Do this project over two days. First, have children paint the plates in steps 1 and 2. When the paint is dry, or on the next day, have them complete the project.

❖ Instead of using brushes to paint their plates, children can dab on paint using sponge squares, crumpled plastic wrap, or *s*-shaped packing peanuts.

❖ In step 5, children can tape the craft spoons to the back of the plate instead of using glue.

Do More
Discuss other jobs people do in a community. Then use these career words to innovate on the rhyme. Write each line of "Rub-a-Dub-Dub" on sentence strips, replacing the words *butcher, baker,* and *candlestick maker* with blank lines. Cut sentence strips to fit the spaces left by each blank and write different careers on the strips. Review these with children. Then hand out the word strips and read the rhyme aloud. When you come to a blank, invite a volunteer to read and place a word strip over the line. After filling in the blank lines, read the revised rhyme together. Repeat using different career word strips.

Follow-the-Directions Art: Nursery Rhymes

Rub-a-Dub-Dub
Rocking Tub

(1) **Paint** one side

of the LARGE folded plate.

Paint it blue to make the sea.

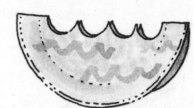

(2) **Paint** one side

of the small half plate

any color you like.

This is the tub.

(3) **Count** three craft spoons.

Draw a face on each.

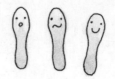

Cut off this bottom strip along the dotted line. Then glue this page to the top of page 32.

31

4

Glue on hair and hats.

Use scrap paper, yarn, and more.

5

Glue the three men

to the unpainted side

of the tub.

6

Stand up the sea.

Put the men in the tub

into the slit.

Tap the sea gently.

See the three men

bob in their tub!

Follow-the-Directions Art: Nursery Rhymes © 2009 by Deborah Schecter, Scholastic Teaching Resources

Jack and Jill

Jack and Jill went up the hill
to fetch a pail of water.
Jack fell down and broke his crown,
and Jill came tumbling after.

What You Need
(for each child)
- Jack and Jill Puppet Slider directions (pages 34-35)
- well and Jack and Jill templates (page 76)
- 9-inch paper plate
- green tempera or watercolor paint
- paint brush
- heavyweight light-blue construction paper, 9 by 12 inches
- stapler
- construction paper in assorted colors
- glue stick
- crayons
- scissors
- large craft stick
- craft materials (optional)

Making the Jack and Jill Puppet Slider

Getting Ready
❖ Each paper plate will make two hills.

❖ Use the templates on page 76 to prepare the construction paper shapes needed to make the well.

❖ Make a class supply of cardstock Jack and Jill templates. Or glue the templates to tagboard and cut them out.

❖ Highlight the word *green* in step 1 using a green marker.

Reading the Rhyme
Read aloud the rhyme. Discuss unfamiliar vocabulary such as *fetch* and *crown*. Then invite pairs of children to take turns acting out the rhyme as the rest of the class reads it together. Afterward, tell children that they are going to make Jack and Jill puppets and a scene for re-enacting the rhyme.

Tips for Success
❖ Do this project over two days. First, have children paint the half plate in step 1. When the paint is dry, or on the next day, have them complete the project.

❖ Before children begin, build vocabulary by reviewing the terms *rectangle* and *triangle*. You might also introduce *semi-circle* (the shape of the hill.)

❖ Check that children glue the well to the hill only, and not the blue paper backing. They should be able to pass the puppet behind the hill.

❖ Invite children to use scrap paper, craft foam, tissue paper, and other craft items to add details to their scenes, such as a sun, clouds, grass, and flowers.

Do More!
Let children use their puppets and background scenes when revisiting the rhyme. Then have them use their projects to practice using positional words and phrases. Invite children to show Jack and Jill *in front of, in back of,* or *beside* the well, for example.

Jack and Jill Puppet Slider

1 **Make** the hill.

$\frac{1}{2}$ **Paint** the half plate green.

Let the paint dry.

2 **Staple** the corners

of the hill

to the bottom

of the blue paper.

3  **Glue** two short strips

to a rectangle.

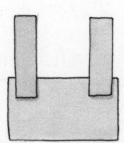

Cut off this bottom strip along the dotted line. Then glue this page to the top of page 35.

Follow-the-Directions Art: Nursery Rhymes © 2009 by Deborah Schecter, Scholastic Teaching Resources

(4) **Turn** the rectangle over.

 Glue a triangle

 to the top of the strips

 This is the well.

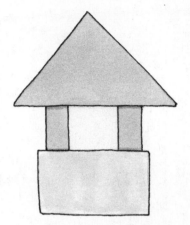

(5)   **Glue** the well to the hill.

(6) **Color** Jack and Jill.

 Glue them to a craft stick.

Slide the craft stick

behind the hill.

Help Jack and Jill

go up and down!

Follow-the-Directions Art: Nursery Rhymes © 2009 by Deborah Schecter, Scholastic Teaching Resources

A Little Bird

. . . .

I saw a little bird, come
hop, hop, hop.
So I said, "Little bird, will you
stop, stop, stop?"
I went to the window to say,
"How do you do?"
But he shook his little tail
and away he flew.

What You Need
(for each child)

- Hop-and-Stop Bird
  directions (pages 37–38)
- 9-inch paper plate
  (uncoated)
- scissors
- hole punch
- brad
- 2 colored reinforcement
  labels
- crayons
- craft materials
  (scrap paper, crayons,
  paint, craft feathers)
- craft glue

Little Jenny Wren

As little Jenny Wren
was sitting by her shed,
she waggled with her tail,
and nodded with her head.
She waggled with her tail,
and nodded with her head,
as little Jenny Wren
was sitting by the shed.

Making the Hop-and-Stop Bird

Getting Ready
You may want to precut the paper plate halves for step 1. If so, have children skip this step.

Reading the Rhyme
Read aloud the rhyme and then invite children to pretend to be the little bird. As you reread it, have them hop, stop, shake their tail, and finally, fly away. Then introduce the craft project by telling children they are going to make little birds with tails that shake.

Tips for Success
❖ Have children use the bottom (convex side) of the plate for the front of their bird.

❖ In step 6, children can cut out a small paper triangle for the bird's beak and a semi-circle for the wing. (Suggest that children glue the beak to the back of the bird for a cleaner look.)

❖ Invite children to decorate their birds using paint, crayons, scrap paper, and craft feathers.

Do More!
To add a movable head to their birds, have children skip step 5. Tell them to cut an additional wedge from the remaining half plate, and then punch a hole in the front of the bird and attach with a brad. Share the rhyme, left, with children and have them use their birds to demonstrate the actions described.

Follow-the-Directions Art: Nursery Rhymes

36

A Little Bird
Hop-and-Stop Bird

1  $\frac{1}{2}$

Fold a paper plate in half.

 Cut the plate on the fold.

2

Make the bird's body.

 Punch a hole near one corner

1 $\frac{1}{2}$

of one half plate.

3

Make the tail.

  **Cut** a wedge

$\frac{1}{2}$

from the other half plate.

 Punch a hole near the point.

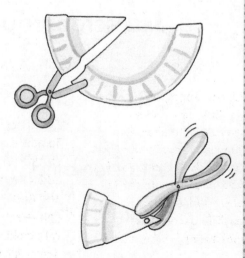

 Cut off this bottom strip along the dotted line. Then glue this page to the top of page 38.

37

4 **Use** a brad

to **put** the tail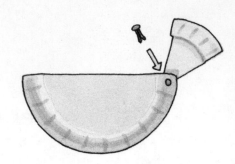

on the body.

5 **Add** an eye.

Use a stick-on paper hole.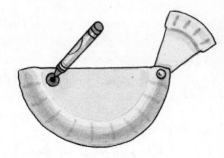

Color in the center.

6   **Cut** out a beak and a wing.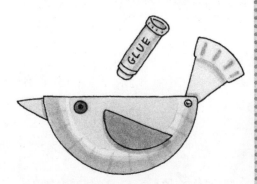

 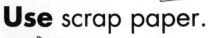 **Use** scrap paper.

Glue them on.

Let your bird

shake its tail—

and then fly away!

Follow-the-Directions Art: Nursery Rhymes © 2009 by Deborah Schecter, Scholastic Teaching Resources

Hickory, Dickory, Dock

Hickory, dickory, dock.
The mouse ran up the clock.
The clock struck one,
the mouse ran down.
Hickory, dickory, dock.

What You Need
(for each child)
- Mouse Clock Climber directions (pages 40–41)
- clock and mouse templates (page 77)
- scissors
- penny
- tape
- length of thin string, 15 inches
- hole punch

Other Materials
- classroom display clock

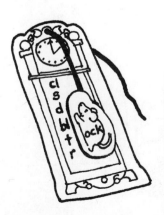

Making the Mouse Clock Climber

Getting Ready
Make a class supply of the clock and mouse templates. Copy the clock onto cardstock and the mouse on regular copy paper. If you cut out the templates for children, have them skip the second part of step 1.

Reading the Rhyme
Read aloud the rhyme once, then reread it, inviting children to use their hands to pantomime the mouse running up and down the clock (their arms). Then tell children that this mouse likes to run up and down the clock on the hour all day long. Show them a classroom display clock. Ask: "What hour on the clock comes after *one*?" Invite a volunteer to tell the new hour and then move the hands to two o'clock. Together, repeat the rhyme substituting the word *two* for *one* as children pantomime the action. Continue in this manner until you've gone full circle around the clock. Then introduce the art project by telling children that they are going to make a mouse that can really run up and down a clock.

Tips for Success
❖ In step 6, assist children in making the knot big enough so that the string cannot slip out of the hole in the clock.

❖ Have children position the mouse nose up when the mouse is running up the clock and then turn it over so it is nose down when descending.

Do More!
Use the clock-climbing mouse to build phonics skills. Make the art project but punch the hole at the top of the clock a bit farther to the right. Write the phonogram *-ock* on the mouse. Revisit the rhyme and ask children to name the words that rhyme (*clock* and *dock*). Ask: "How are these two words alike and different?" (same *-ock* ending, different beginnings). Together make a list of other *-ock* words (*tock, lock, rock, sock, block*). Write the onsets on the left side of the clock. Invite volunteers to make the mouse climb slowly as the rest of the class reads aloud each new word that is formed.

Hickory, Dickory, Dock
Mouse Clock Climber

1 **Color** the clock

and the mouse.

Cut them out.

---

2 **Turn** the mouse over.

  1

Tape a penny to one side.

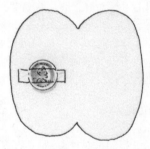

 1

3 **Tape** one end of the string

to the other side.

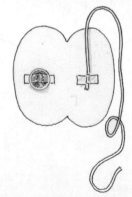

 2

4 **Fold** the two sides together.

Tape closed.

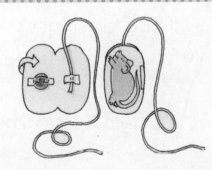

Cut off this bottom strip along the dotted line. Then glue this page to the top of page 41.

Follow-the-Directions Art: Nursery Rhymes © 2009 by Deborah Schecter, Scholastic Teaching Resources

(5) **Punch** a hole

○

in the circle

at the top of the clock.

(6) **Poke** the other end

of the string

through the hole.

Knot the end.

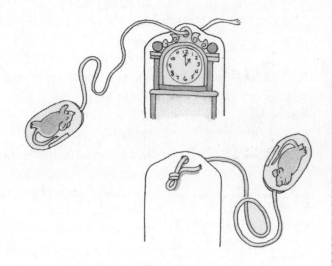

Pull the string from the back.

Then let it go.

Watch your mouse run

up and down the clock!

The Queen of Hearts

The Queen of Hearts,
she made some tarts,
all on a summer's day.
The Knave of Hearts,
he stole the tarts,
and with them ran away.

The King of Hearts
called for the tarts,
and scolded the Knave full score.
The Knave of Hearts
brought back the tarts,
and vowed he'd steal no more.

What You Need
(for each child)
- Royal Crown directions (pages 43–44)
- heart templates (page 78)
- colored paper in assorted colors, patterns, and textures
- 3 trays or resealable plastic bags
- bordette strip, 24 inches long
- craft glue
- craft materials (pompoms, dot stickers, glitter glue, craft foam, sequins, plastic gems)

Making the Royal Crown

Getting Ready
Use the three heart templates on page 78 to make a large quantity of paper hearts in different colors, patterns and textures for children to choose from. Examples might include construction paper, tissue paper, gift wrap, and wallpaper samples. Place the hearts, according to size, in separate trays or in resealable plastic bags.

Reading the Rhyme
Read aloud the rhyme and discuss unfamiliar words and phrases, such as *tart* (a pastry similar to a small pie), *knave* (a servant or someone who is tricky or dishonest), *full score* (20 times), and *vowed* (promised). Reread the rhyme and then discuss what happens in the poem. Ask children what they think of the knave's behavior. Why did he return the tarts? Did he learn a lesson? Discuss honesty and why it is important. Then tell children that they are going to make a royal crown of hearts to wear when revisiting the rhyme.

Tips for Success
❖ Before children begin, review the concept of repeating patterns, and provide a few examples.

❖ To build math vocabulary, show children the three heart templates. Review the terms *small*, *medium*, and *large*.

❖ Make sure children let the glue dry completely before putting on their crowns.

❖ Assist children in fitting the crowns to their heads and stapling them closed.

Do More!
To help children learn and practice the words for different shapes, have them make crowns for the Queen of Triangles or the King of Circles! Use the templates on page 78 to prepare an assortment of shapes in different sizes (squares, rectangles, triangles, circles, diamonds). Review the name for each shape. Then invite children to make another patterned crown using one of the new shapes.

Follow-the-Directions Art: Nursery Rhymes

The Queen of Hearts
Royal Crown

1 **Choose** some LARGE paper hearts,

medium hearts, and small hearts.

Choose different colors, too.

2 **Practice** making a pattern

on the curvy strip.

Use hearts in different

sizes and colors.

3 **Glue** the hearts

to the curvy strip.

 Cut off this bottom strip along the dotted line. Then glue this page to the top of page 44.

4 How else will you

decorate your crown?

Use pompoms, dot stickers,

glitter glue, and more.

5 **Fit** the crown

to your head.

Staple it closed.

Wear your royal crown!
Are you the Queen of Hearts
or the King of Hearts?

Follow-the-Directions Art: Nursery Rhymes © 2009 by Deborah Schecter, Scholastic Teaching Resources

The Old Woman Who Lived in a Shoe

There was an old woman
who lived in a shoe.
She had so many children,
she didn't know what to do.

She gave them some broth
along with some bread,
then hugged them all soundly
and sent them to bed.

What You Need
(for each child)
- Lace-Up Shoe directions (pages 46–47)
- shoe template (page 79)
- scissors
- hole punch
- 10 colored reinforcement labels
- crayons
- length of yarn, about 1 yard

Other Materials
- string
- tape

Name: Andrew

How Many Bears Will Fit in the Shoe?

How many I think will fit: 30

How many fit: 14

Making the Lace-Up Shoe

Getting Ready
❖ Copy the shoe templates onto cardstock or glue to cardboard. You may want to cut out the shoes ahead of time. If you do this, have children skip step 1.

❖ Wrap tape around the ends of the yarn to make lacing the shoe easier. (Or dip the ends in glue and let dry.)

❖ Tape several string outlines of the Old Woman's shoe on the floor. Make them big enough so that small groups of children can sit or stand in them. (See Reading the Rhyme, below.)

Reading the Rhyme
Read aloud the rhyme and have children join in as you read it again. Then invite children to act out the rhyme. Divide the class into small groups. Let one child in each group be the Old Woman. He or she goes around to the other children in the group, pretending to give them broth and bread, as well as a hug. Each child in turn then goes inside the shoe and "falls asleep." Then tell children that they are going to make a lace-up shoe like the Old Woman's home.

Tips for Success
❖ Before lacing the shoe, have children adjust the two lengths of yarn so they are about equal.

❖ If children need help, assist them in lacing up their shoe and tying a bow.

❖ Invite children to take their shoes home to practice tying with family members.

Do More!
How many children (or teddy bear counters!) will fit in a shoe? Help children find out and build estimation and counting skills. Create a recording sheet as shown, left, using a shoe template. Make multiple copies. Place these at a center with a supply of teddy bear counters and a real shoe. When children visit the center, they estimate and write on a recording sheet the number of counters they think will fit in the shoe. Next, they fill up the shoe with counters, and then count and record the actual number. To extend, provide smaller and larger shoes and repeat the activity. Encourage children to use the results from the first activity as they make their new estimates.

Lace-Up Shoe

1 ✂ 👢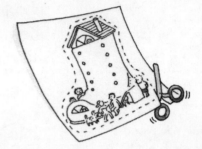

Cut out the shoe.

2 **Punch** a hole in each

10 ○

of the ten circles.

3 **Count** ten **10**

stick-on paper holes.

Stick one over each hole. **1**

Follow-the-Directions Art: Nursery Rhymes © 2009 by Deborah Schecter, Scholastic Teaching Resources

✂ Cut off this bottom strip along the dotted line. Then glue this page to the top of page 47.

4 **Color** the shoe.

5 **Turn** the shoe over.

Thread the ends of the yarn

2

through the bottom two holes.

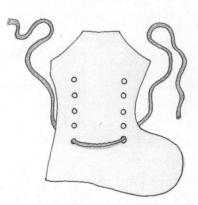

6 **Turn** the shoe

to the front.

Now, lace up the shoe.
Tie a bow at the top!

Follow-the-Directions Art: Nursery Rhymes © 2009 by Deborah Schecter, Scholastic Teaching Resources

Baa, Baa, Black Sheep

"Baa, Baa, Black sheep have you any wool?"

"Yes sir, yes sir, three bags full.

One for my master.
One for my dame.
And one for the little boy who lives down the lane."

What You Need
(for each child)
- Speaking Sheep Puppet directions (pages 49–50)
- two 6-inch paper plates (uncoated)
- 3 cotton balls
- construction paper, assorted colors
- scissors
- craft glue
- 2 self-adhesive wiggle eyes
- 1 pompom
- crayons
- stapler

Other Materials
- 3 paper lunch bags
- newspaper

Making the Speaking Sheep Puppet

Getting Ready
❖ Highlight the word *red* in step 3 using a red colored pencil.

❖ Stuff three paper lunch bags with newspaper and twist them closed.

Reading the Rhyme
Read the rhyme aloud and invite children to join in as you reread it. Then let volunteers take turns playing the part of the sheep, the master, dame, and little boy. (Change the word *boy* to *girl* as appropriate.) Give the "sheep" the three "bags of wool" (the stuffed bags). While the class reads the rhyme again, the sheep gives each bag of wool to the correct person. For more counting practice, prepare additional bags and innovate on the text, for example: "Yes sir, yes sir, six bags full. One for my master. Two for my dame. And three for the little boy who lives down the lane." Then tell children that they are going to make sheep puppets that can speak just like the sheep in the rhyme can.

Tips for Success
❖ In steps 1–3, have children use the bottom (convex side) of the plate to make the sheep's face.

❖ Instead of using wiggle eyes, children can make the sheep's eyes using dot stickers or scrap paper.

❖ In step 4, model how to fold the second plate with the bottom (convex side) facing out.

Do More!
Let children use their sheep puppets to revisit the rhyme and take turns speaking the sheep's lines. Then have them use the puppets for more math practice. Write the rhyme on sentence strips and replace the number words with blank lines. Cut a blank sentence strip to fit the space left by each blank, and write different numbers on each. Insert different number combinations into the rhyme. Have children check that the numbers add up correctly. Then reread the rhyme and let children take turns using their sheep's mouth to pick up and hand out in turn the corresponding number of bags.

Follow-the-Directions Art: Nursery Rhymes

Baa, Baa, Black Sheep
Speaking Sheep Puppet

1 **3** **Glue** three cotton balls

to the rim of a paper plate.

2 **Cut** out two paper ears.

Glue them on.

3 **2** **Glue** on two wiggle eyes

 and a pompom nose.

Draw on a red smile.

4 **Fold** the other plate in half. $\frac{1}{2}$

Then **unfold** it.

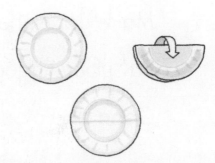

 Cut off this bottom strip along the dotted line. Then glue this page to the top of page 50.

5 **Stack** the plates.

 **Put** the sheep face on top.

6 **Staple** the bottom halves $\frac{1}{2}$

of the plates together.

7 **Fold** down the loose half $\frac{1}{2}$

of the bottom plate.

Make your sheep speak!

Put your fingers inside the back.

Open and close your hand.

Follow-the-Directions Art: Nursery Rhymes © 2009 by Deborah Schecter, Scholastic Teaching Resources

50

Humpty Dumpty

Humpty Dumpty sat on a wall.
Humpty Dumpty had a great fall.
All the king's horses
and all the king's men
couldn't put Humpty together again.

What You Need
(for each child)
- Roly-Poly directions
  (pages 52–53)
- large plastic egg
- walnut-sized lump of clay
- 2 wiggle eyes
- permanent markers
- two construction paper
  strips, 1/2-inch by 3 inches
- two construction paper
  strips, 1/2-inch by 5 inches
- one piece of bow-tie pasta
- 1/2-inch glue dots or clear
  tape

Making the Roly-Poly

Getting Ready
If children want to paint the pasta bow-ties, have them do this ahead of time and let the paint dry completely before affixing to the eggs.

Reading the Rhyme
Read the rhyme aloud and invite children to chime in as you reread it. Invite children to make up simple hand motions to act it out. For example, they might make a fist to show Humpty when he is whole, then show him falling and spread out their fingers to show him breaking into pieces.

Show children a plastic egg. Ask them what they think will happen when you stand it on a desk. (*It will fall over or roll away.*) Then tell them that they are each going to make a Humpty Dumpty egg that will not fall!

Tips for Success
❖ Children may need to adjust the position of the clay in the bottom of the egg to make it stand upright. (Humpty stands because the added weight in the bottom of the egg lowers the egg's center of gravity.)

❖ Instead of using wiggle eyes, children can use large dot stickers and add pupils with a marker, or simply draw them on using a permanent marker.

❖ Have children practice using glue dots with scrap paper. (Or, have children use clear tape instead of glue dots.)

Do More!
Invite children to create a wall for their Humpty to sit on. Collect an assortment of small empty cartons, such as tea cartons or animal cracker boxes. Have children cover the boxes with brown packing paper and then use small sponge rectangles and tempera paint to stamp brick shapes in a pattern on the paper. When the paint is dry, children can sit Humpty on the wall and watch him not fall!

Humpty Dumpty
Roly-Poly

1 **Open** the egg.

 Press a lump of clay

 into the bottom.

Close the egg.

2  **Make** the face.

 2 **Stick** on two wiggle eyes.

 Draw a mouth.

3 **2** **Count** two L O N G and

2  two short paper strips.

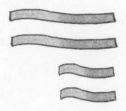

 Cut off this bottom strip along the dotted line. Then glue this page to the top of page 53.

Follow-the-Directions Art: Nursery Rhymes © 2009 by Deborah Schecter, Scholastic Teaching Resources

4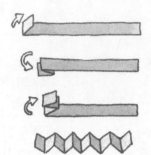

Fold each strip

back and forth.

5

Add arms to the egg.

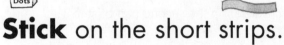

Stick on the short strips.

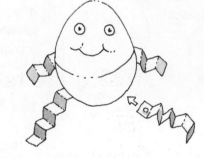

6

Add legs to the egg.

Stick on the L O N G strips.

7

Stick on a pasta bow tie!

Will Humpty fall?

Place him on your desk.

What happens?

Follow-the-Directions Art: Nursery Rhymes © 2009 by Deborah Schecter, Scholastic Teaching Resources

A Tisket, A Tasket

A tisket, a tasket,
a green and yellow basket.
I wrote a letter to my love,
and on the way I dropped it,

I dropped it,
I dropped it,
and on the way I dropped it.

What You Need
(for each child)
- Fold-Up Basket directions (pages 55–56)
- basket template, page 80
- crayons
- scissors
- hole punch
- stapler
- pipe cleaner
- glue dots, glue sticks, or tape

Making the Fold-Up Basket

Getting Ready
❖ To make bigger baskets, enlarge the template by 150% when photocopying.

❖ You may want to precut the basket templates for children ahead of time. If you do this, have children skip the second part of step 1.

Reading the Rhyme
After sharing the rhyme with children, let them take turns pantomiming the action in the poem. Then ask them about the letter: What was written in the letter? What might have happened to it? Did someone find it and pick it up? Did the letter ever get where it was supposed to go? Invite children to describe or act out different scenarios. Then tell children that they are going to make a basket and write a letter to put in it.

Tips for Success
❖ In step 3, have children use the dotted lines on the decorated side of the basket template as a guide when folding in the flaps.

❖ Instead of stapling the basket together, children might use glue dots, glue sticks, or tape.

❖ To enhance the handle made in step 7, show children how to wrap the pipe cleaner around a pencil to create a spiral and then stretch it out a bit to attach it to the basket.

Dear _Aunt Diane_ ,

A tisket, a tasket,

a _pink_ and _orange_ basket!

This letter is from me to you.

to say I like you—I really do!

From _Sarah_

Do More!
Copy the fill-in letter-poem, left, and photocopy a class set. Help children fill in the name of a friend or family member on the top line, write the colors they used to decorate their basket (or use crayons to indicate the colors) on the lines in the rhyme, and sign their name on the bottom line. Then have children fold it up, place it inside their basket, and send their letter by "basket-delivery!"

Follow-the-Directions Art: Nursery Rhymes

A Tisket, A Tasket
Fold-Up Basket

1

Color the basket template.

Cut it out.

2

Punch a hole at each circle. ◯

3

Turn the template over.

Fold in the flaps.

Then **unfold**.

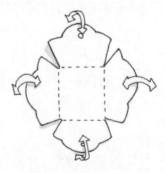

4

Lift up one flap. 1

Cut off this bottom strip along the dotted line. Then glue this page to the top of page 56.

55

Follow-the-Directions Art: Nursery Rhymes © 2009 by Deborah Schecter, Scholastic Teaching Resources

5   **Overlap** the flaps

on each side.

Staple closed.

6   **Do** the same thing

on the other side.

7   **Poke** the ends

of a pipe cleaner

through the holes.

Bend up the ends.

A tisket, a tasket,

put a letter in your basket!

Follow-the-Directions Art: Nursery Rhymes © 2009 by Deborah Schecter, Scholastic Teaching Resources

Daffy-Down-Dilly

. . . .

Daffy-down-dilly
has just come to town
with a petticoat green
and a bright yellow gown.
And her white blossoms
are peeping around.

What You Need
(for each child)
- Dandy Daffodil directions (pages 58–59)
- yellow paper baking cup
- scissors
- white paper baking cup
- craft glue
- green pipe cleaner
- green paper
- clear tape

Making the Dandy Daffodil

Getting Ready
❖ You may want to prepare the yellow baking cup cones ahead of time. If so, have children skip steps 1 and 2.

❖ Highlight the color words *yellow* and *green* in steps 1 and 5–7 using markers in corresponding colors.

Reading the Rhyme
Read aloud the rhyme and ask children what they think the poem might be about (*a girl or lady wearing a brightly colored gown and petticoat*). Then show children a real or artificial daffodil that has a yellow center and white petals (or a photo of one). Explain that the poem is about a daffodil that has just bloomed (*just come to town*). What part of the flower might be the "petticoat green"? (*the stem*). The "bright yellow gown"? (*the cup-shaped part of the flower*) Last, point out the "white blossoms" that "are peeping around." (*the petals*) Then tell children that they are going to create a daffodil like the one described in the rhyme.

Tips for Success
❖ In step 1, have children flatten the baking cup before cutting.

❖ In step 4, model for children how to squeeze just one drop of glue onto the white baking cup.

❖ In step 5, children will flatten the point at the bottom of the yellow cone as they press it into the glue.

Do More!
Use this rhyme's title, "Daffy-Down-Dilly," to introduce alliteration. Write the title on chart paper. Ask children what they notice about the words. Guide them to recognize that the words all start with the same consonant sound. Invite children to use alliteration to extend the title into a sentence, for example, *Daffy-Down-Dilly dips and dances in the dew at dawn*, or *Daffy-Down-Dilly dines on a dish of doughnuts for dessert*. Encourage children to look for more examples of alliteration in other nursery rhymes and stories they read.

Follow-the-Directions Art: Nursery Rhymes

Daffy-Down-Dilly
Dandy Daffodil

1 ✂ 🧁 $\frac{1}{2}$

Cut a yellow baking cup in half.

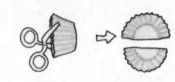

2 📜 1 $\frac{1}{2}$

Roll one half

🔻

into a cone.

📼

Tape it closed.

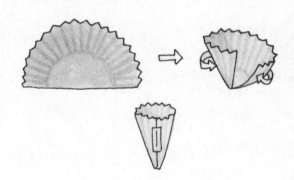

3 ✂

Make cuts

all around the sides

of a white baking cup.

4

Put a drop of glue

in the middle.

✂ Cut off this bottom strip along the dotted line. Then glue this page to the top of page 59.

Follow-the-Directions Art: Nursery Rhymes © 2009 by Deborah Schecter, Scholastic Teaching Resources

5 **Press** the bottom

of the yellow cone

into the glue. Let dry.

6 **Tape** a green pipe cleaner

to the back of the flower.

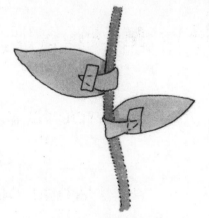

7   **Tear** or **cut** leaves

from green paper.

Tape them to the stem.

What part of your daffodil

is the petticoat?

What part is the gown?

Mary, Mary, Quite Contrary

Mary, Mary, quite contrary,
how does your garden grow?
"With silver bells and cockle shells,
and pretty maids all in a row."

What You Need
(for each child)

Silver Bells
- Silver Bells directions (pages 61–62)
- paper-lined foil baking cup
- sharpened pencil
- green pipe cleaner
- large silver jingle bell (12 mm. size)
- green paper
- scissors
- tape

Cockle Shells
- Cockle Shells directions (pages 63–64)
- paper baking cup
- green pipe cleaner
- tape
- green paper
- scissors
- crayons or paint

Other Materials
- small bell and cockle shell (or photos of each)

Making the Silver Bells and Cockle Shells

Getting Ready
❖ For the Silver Bells project, leave the paper liners inside the foil baking cups for added durability,

❖ You may want to poke the hole in the foil cups ahead of time. If so, have children skip step 1.

❖ Use a light green marker to highlight the word *green* in steps 2 and 6 of the Silver Bells directions and in steps 2 and 4 of the Cockle Shells directions.

Reading the Rhyme
Read aloud the rhyme. Discuss words that may be unfamiliar to children, such as *contrary* (stubborn or difficult). Then ask children if they think the flowers in this garden are real or imaginary. (If possible, let children examine a real bell and a real cockle shell, or photos of each.) Read aloud the rhyme again, substituting the names of children in your class for *Mary*. When you reach the third line, invite the child whose name is being used to say the kinds of flowers—real or imaginary—that are growing in his or her garden. Then tell children that they are going to make the imaginary flowers in this rhyme.

Tips for Success
❖ In step 2 of the Silver Bells project, children may need help poking the pipe cleaner through the loop in the jingle bell.

❖ In step 3, check that children bend just the tip of the pipe cleaner. This will ensure that in step 4 the jingle bell fits snugly inside the baking cup.

Do More!
Set up a flower-making center. Stock the center with a variety of craft materials, such as colored tissue paper, paper baking cups, pipe cleaners, decorative paper scraps, craft foam, assorted dried pasta shapes, and glue. Invite children to visit the center to design and create their own imaginary flowers.

Follow-the-Directions Art: Nursery Rhymes

Silver Bells

1 **Poke** a tiny hole

in the middle

of a foil baking cup.

Use a pencil.

2 **Poke** a green pipe cleaner

through the loop

of a jingle bell.

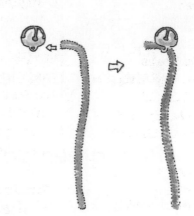

3 **Bend** the tip

of the pipe cleaner.

Cut off this bottom strip along the dotted line. Then glue this page to the top of page 62.

4 **Poke** the other end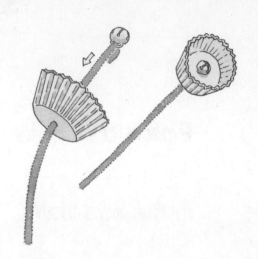

of the pipe cleaner

through the hole

in the baking cup.

5 **Bend** down the pipe cleaner.

6

Tear or **cut** leaves

from green paper.

Tape them to the stem.

Ring-a-ling! Ring-a-ling!

Silver bells are singing!

1 **Flatten** a paper baking cup.

$\frac{1}{2}$

Fold it in half.

2 **Tape** one end $\frac{1}{1}$

of a green pipe cleaner

to the middle of one side.

3 **Fold** the baking cup in half. $\frac{1}{2}$

Tape it closed.

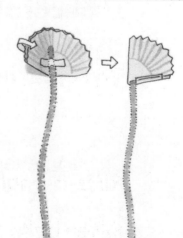

Cut off this bottom strip along the dotted line. Then glue this page to the top of page 64.

 Glue this page to the bottom of page 63.

4

Tear or **cut** leaves

from green paper.

5

Tape the leaves

to the stem.

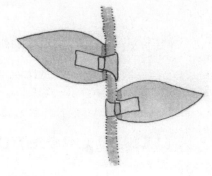

6

Use crayons or paint

to **decorate** your flower.

Did you ever see a flower

that looks like a shell?

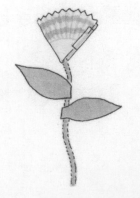

Follow-the-Directions Art: Nursery Rhymes © 2009 by Deborah Schecter, Scholastic Teaching Resources

Higglety, Pigglety

Higglety, pigglety, my black hen,
she lays eggs for gentlemen.
Gentlemen come every day
to see what my black hen did lay.
Sometimes nine, and sometimes ten,
Higglety, pigglety, my black hen.

What You Need
(for each child)
- Nesting Hen directions (pages 66–67)
- construction paper circle, 3 1/4 inches
- construction paper scraps
- scissors
- craft glue
- 2 colored reinforcement labels
- crayons
- pencil
- craft feather
- paper baking cup
- 10 yogurt raisins

Other Materials
- 10 plastic eggs
- basket

Making the Nesting Hen

Getting Ready
❖ Prepare the paper circles ahead of time, using different colors for children to choose from.

❖ Gather ten plastic eggs and a basket for use in Reading the Rhyme, below.

Reading the Rhyme
Place nine plastic eggs in the basket. Then read aloud the rhyme and invite children to join in as you reread it. Show children the basket of eggs. Together count the eggs. Then ask, "What if the hen laid ten eggs? How many more eggs would we need to add?" Continue this process, starting with a given number of eggs and adding or taking away different amounts. Afterward, tell children that they are going to make a hen and her nest of eggs.

Tips for Success
❖ Before children begin the project, build vocabulary by reviewing the terms *circle* and *triangle*.

❖ When affixing the beak, have children glue it under the fold for a cleaner look.

❖ Instead of yogurt raisins, children can use clay to form the ten eggs for the hen's nest.

Do More!
Use the nesting hens with children to practice counting and simple addition and subtraction skills. Begin by having children count and place a given number of eggs in their nest, for example, four. Then tell them that their hen laid two more eggs. How many eggs did she lay in all? Have children use their extra eggs to find the answer. Or start with six eggs in the nest. Tell children that the hen gave away three eggs. How many eggs are left?

Higglety, Pigglety
Nesting Hen

(1) **Choose** a paper circle.

 Fold it in half. $\frac{1}{2}$

 This is your hen.

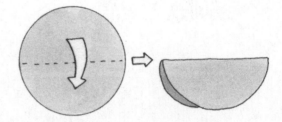

(2) **Make** a beak.

Cut a small paper triangle.

Glue it under the fold.

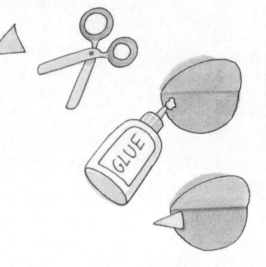

(3) **Add** eyes.

 Use two **2** stick-on paper holes.

Color in the centers.

 Cut off this bottom strip along the dotted line. Then glue this page to the top of page 67.

66

Follow-the-Directions Art: Nursery Rhymes © 2009 by Deborah Schecter, Scholastic Teaching Resources

(4) **Draw** on wings.

(5) **Add** a tail.

Use a pencil to **poke**

a small **hole in the fold.**

Stick in a craft feather.

 10

Count ten yogurt raisins.

Place them

in a paper baking cup.

Sit your hen

on her eggs

in the nest!

Initial Cake Templates

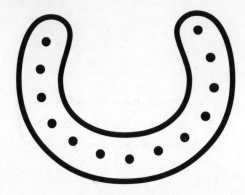

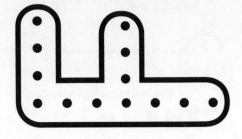

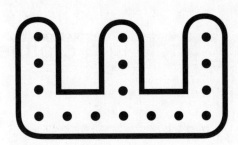

Initial Cake Templates

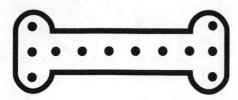

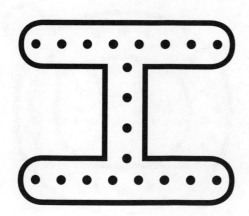

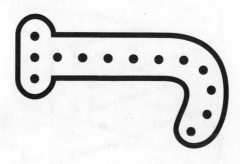

Initial Cake Templates

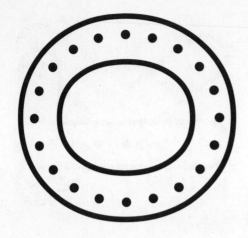 

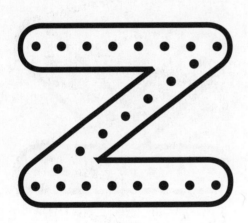 

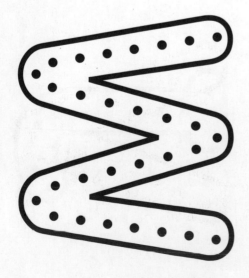 

Follow-the-Directions Art: Nursery Rhymes © 2009 by Deborah Schecter, Scholastic Teaching Resources

Initial Cake Templates

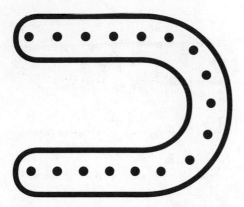

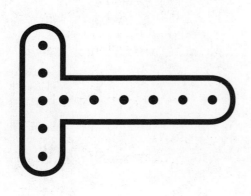

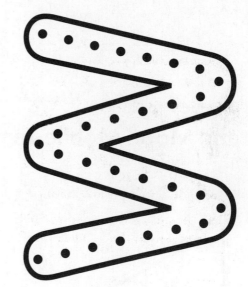

Initial Cake Templates

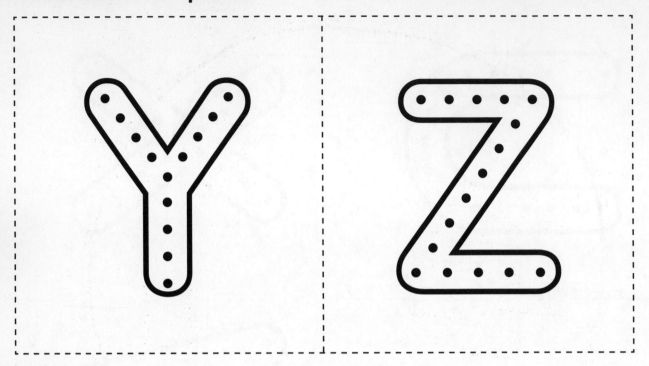

Cow and Moon Mobile Templates

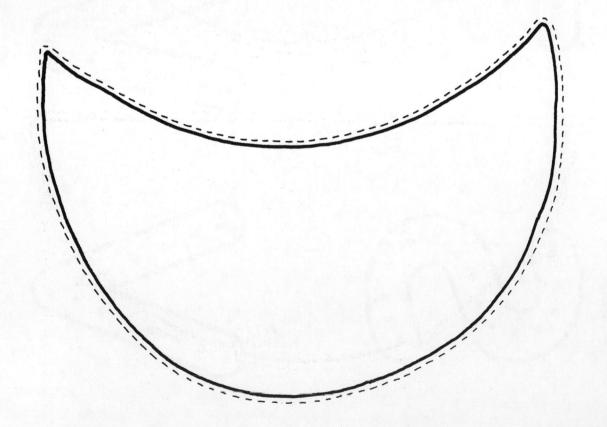

Cow and Moon Mobile Templates

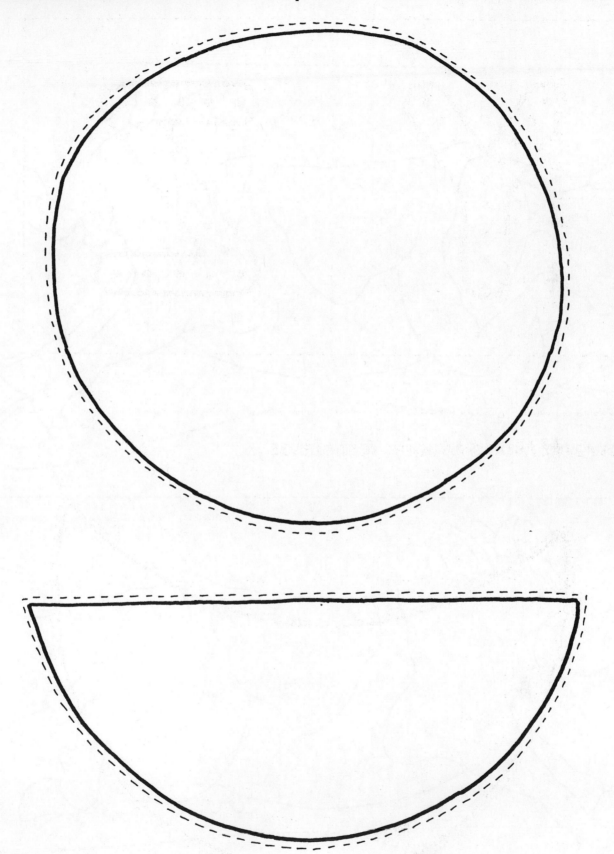

Cow and Moon Mobile Templates

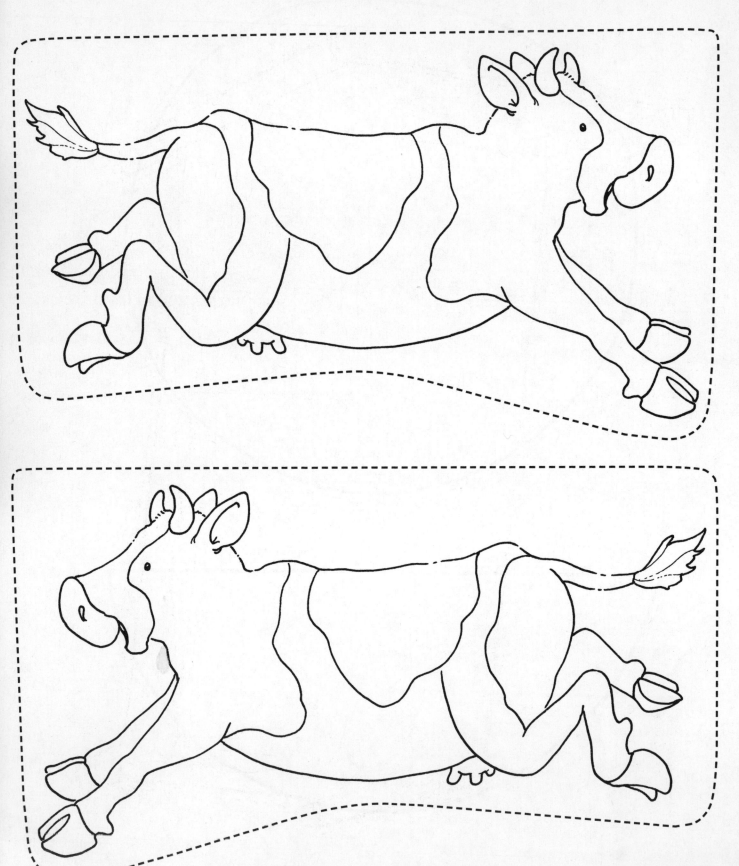

Follow-the-Directions Art: Nursery Rhymes © 2009 by Deborah Schecter, Scholastic Teaching Resources

Cozy Quilt Template

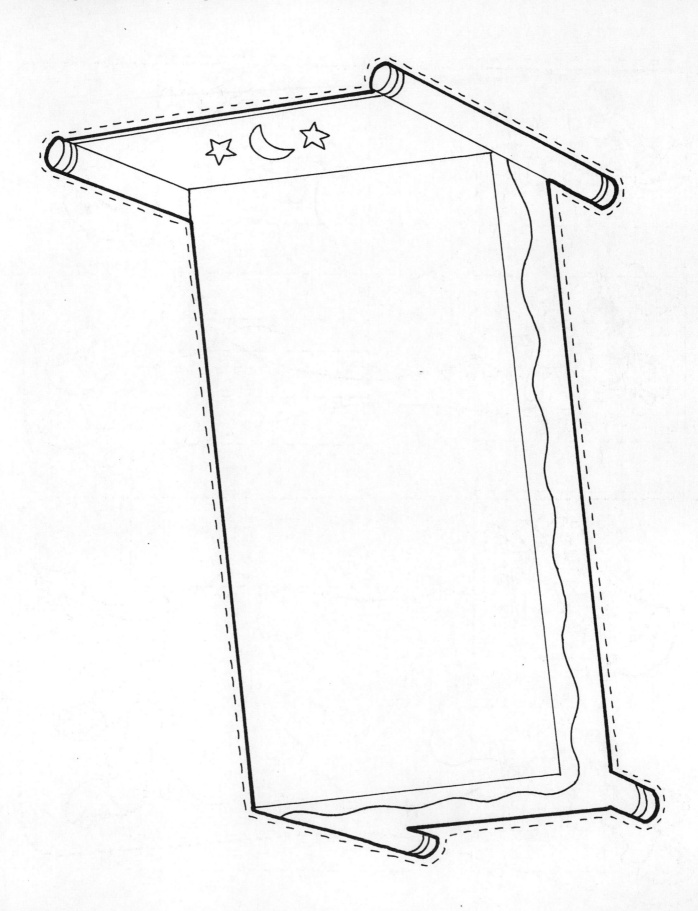

Jack and Jill Puppet Slider and Well Templates

Follow-the-Directions Art: Nursery Rhymes © 2009 by Deborah Schecter, Scholastic Teaching Resources

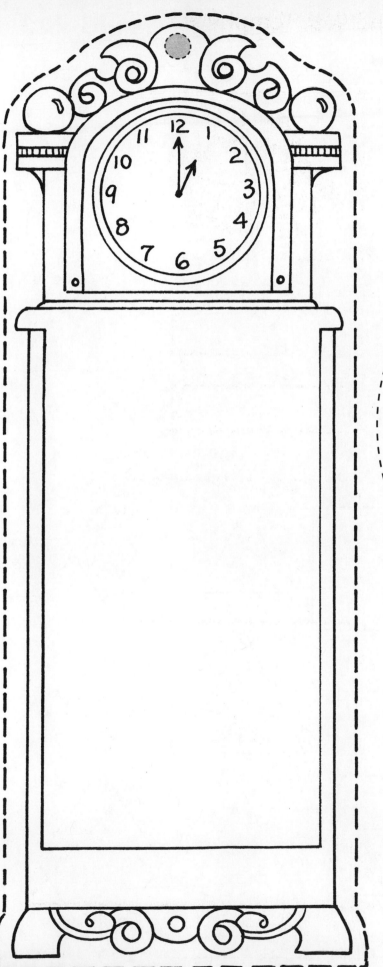

Mouse Clock Climber
Templates

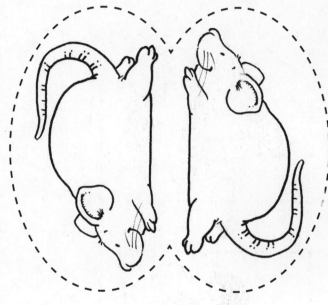

Royal Crown Templates

Lace-Up Shoe Template

Fold-Up Basket Template

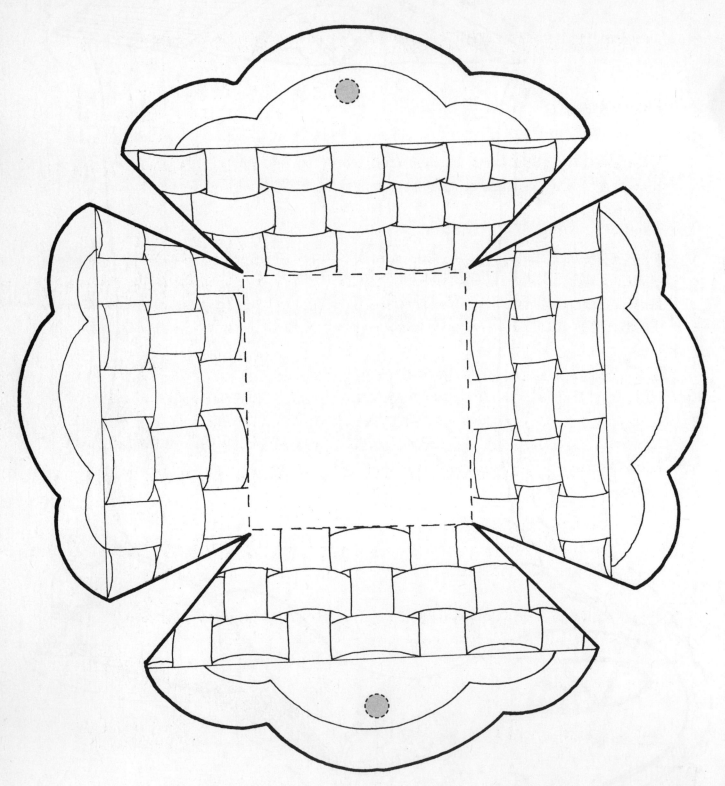

Follow-the-Directions Art: Nursery Rhymes © 2009 by Deborah Schecter, Scholastic Teaching Resources